People of Purpose:

Embracing Your Uniqueness Changes the World

L. J. Boulding

People of Purpose: Embracing Your Uniqueness Changes the World

Quote in chapter five -- c.1599-1601, William Shakespeare, *Hamlet*, Act I, Scene III.

Quote in chapter eight from Dr. Lance Wallnau, (Speaker and Business Consultant, Lance Learning Group, www.lancewallnau.com). Used by permission.

ISBN-10: 0692633774
ISBN-13: 978-0692633779

DEDICATION

I dedicate this book to God without whom it would not have been possible.

To each of my readers for taking the time to read God's heart to you.

To my friends and sisters Apostle Cassandra Bennett, Apostle Cheree Garner, Pastor Gloria Hawkins, and Juateen Allen for encouragement, prayers, and inspiriting me to let God's light shine through me.

To my brothers Pastor Aaron Price, Charles Lackey Jr., Harold Jackson, John Williams, and Novatus Valentine for giving me the inspiration to live this journey and go for it.

To Apostle Daryl Davis and Bishop William Goodman who taught me many valuable lessons through the word of God and by their lifestyles.

To Chandler Bolt for assisting me with the vehicle to make my dreams come true.

To R. E. Vance my writing coach who mentored and encouraged me through every step of the process.

To everyone else for being such an integral, impactful part of my life.

Bless you Family.

Love you much!

Contents

FOREWORD

There are many who have attempted to answer questions or discuss the whys and hows of embracing purpose. This work gives voice to Godly answers written for our good in the word of God, the Bible.

It is written, "And I am convinced and sure this very thing. He who began a good work in you will continue until the day of Jesus Christ [right up to the time of his return], developing [that good work], perfecting and bringing it to full completion in you" Philippians 1:6 (AMP).

"[Not in your own strength] effectually at work in you [energizing and creating in you the power and desire], both to will and to work for His good pleasure, satisfaction, and delight." Philippians 2:13 (AMP) (cp. Ephesians 2:10 AMP).

This book discusses, through the heart of His humble servant, the uniqueness of the process by which God, the Holy Spirit, uses to mature His sons and daughters. Between each line of pain, glory, or trial, various opinions, betrayal, separation, and rejection; comes healing, blessing, surrender, appreciation, love, maturity, and acceleration toward personal victory and purpose.

These pages share how surrender to the LORD Jesus and His

purpose for our lives will forge metal in us—a will to be steadfast and committed to the process of maturity. It was sung years ago and declared, "Through it all. I've learned to trust in Jesus. I've learned to trust in God."

It is shared and I concur. There is a uniqueness to the walk we have with God through Jesus Christ that is exclusively our own. We are in covenant with the Father through Him. He loves us all individually and collectively.

The author takes us on her journey of walking with God. She shares how He will bring us to triumph in Him through what He has started in us. He will continue to work His will and purpose through us uniquely for the good of His body (the body of Christ). He helps us come to know that although we are part of a whole, that our individual gifts, talents, education, and skills are added to the whole to fulfill His purpose in the earth.

Through every failure, setback, and triumph, we are drawn closer to the Father by His love for us. He longs for us to abide in Him and find pleasure in His presence near His Person.

This is where purpose is revealed, in His presence. We learn in His presence He loves us. He is faithful to us. He pours out His Grace upon us. He is committed to us. He will never leave us nor forsake us (Hebrews 13:5b). And He will bring His best out of us that we may uniquely glorify Him in the earth.

Ultimately, God has made you a personal person. He gave you an identity. He wants us all to know we have DNA in Him through Christ Jesus. The world needs to see His Light in YOU! "...that they may see YOUR good work and glorify your Father which is in Heaven" Matthew 5:16.

These shared pages will help you understand you are fearfully and wonderfully made (Psalm 139:14).

You are called according to His purpose for your life. You were raised up for such a time as this. Embrace who it is that GOD is making you.

My prayer is that you find within these pages as I have a greater love for God, the appreciation for the process, and the purpose of your sonship you're looking for. I pray you find this book to greatly assist you in your quest for purpose in God. Embrace your purpose. Pursue it in Him. It's uniquely YOURS!

Bishop William Goodman

INTRODUCTION

Congratulations on being obedient to the Holy Spirit's leading to read this book. This is my story on how I was led to find my purpose and embrace my uniqueness.

It started out as a few catch phrases that the Father led me to add on my Facebook page every morning for a couple of weeks. He would have me write things like, "People of purpose and destiny pursue the will of God, not the will of man." "People of purpose embrace their uniqueness while expressing their God-given talents." Or, "People of purpose trust the Lord to honor His promises found in His word."

I was shocked at the many positive responses and that the number of likes were increasing on my page. I knew it was not by my doing, but God was drawing my Facebook friends to read His words that would influence their minds to think differently.

Shortly after the posts on Facebook, I was led to just start writing things down as the inspiration hit me. One morning as I was in my quiet place with God, I was led to call my old pastor. As soon as she heard my voice she said, "I was just thinking about you as I read this Scripture, *'For a great door and effectual door is opened unto me, and there are many adversaries' — 1 Corinthians 16:9.*"

Not long after she gave me that Scripture, God opened a huge door of opportunity for me to be able to enroll in a writing school. There I learned what it would take for me to fulfill my lifelong dream of becoming a writer and published author. It also gave me the opportunity to flow in my purpose to produce what you now hold in your hands.

In this book I share some delightful stories, lessons learned along the way, and the many obstacles that I faced to get to the end of this phase of my journey. The seed of purpose is cultivated and its results is released over various periods of time according to God's master plan.

I want you to know that you didn't just happen to discover this book to read, but you were divinely appointed to do so just like I was divinely appointed to write it. Everything has a purpose and a time to manifest in the earth (Ecclesiastes 3:1-10). This is my set time to manifest that which God has put in me to reach you. No matter when the book was written, the Father controls the time of the people destined and appointed to read it.

This book was developed to be a mini training manual to assist you along your way. As you go through the pages, you will learn about many of the things you will encounter while fulfilling your purpose and displaying your divine uniqueness. In all things, I've learned to give God all the glory for everything that He allows to come and go in my life. This is a strategic weapon against the attacks of the enemy.

Even the enemy has a purpose. I consider him my teacher in spiritual warfare and faith building. He teaches my hands to fight and my fingers to war (Psalm 144:1). He also assists me with total dependence and trust in God to fight the battle through me in His strength with guaranteed success one hundred percent of the time.

You must believe that your unique purpose will not and cannot be supplied by anyone else. He made you and is maturing you to bring forth that which He desires to display at any given moment. You have been living your purpose and touching lives with the essence of your presence since the day you were conceived in your mother's womb.

Every person who has crossed your path has been changed whether impactful or in a minute way, but nevertheless they will not be the same. God is teaching me to look past the obvious and see Him in all things. He is revealing more of the mind of Christ and how to walk in it every day.

I promise you as you continue reading through the pages of this book, you will not think the same, nor will you be the same person as when you started. There is a transformation designed to happen to you through the words in this book. He has purposed to wash you with the water of His words that will come to you while you read and study this book.

As children of God, we have to stay prayed up and keep an open mind. While you read the words on these pages, it is my prayer that they will become spirit, life, and flesh to you (John 6:63).

The Father has graced me to now know that I have a unique voice that must be released into the earth for such a time as this. It is my hope that you too will discover your voice and unique messages by the time you have finished this book.

What I discuss in this book is what helped me achieve one of my lifetime goals and pave the way for the discipline needed to be successful in other areas of my life. After reading this book, you will have the momentum you will need to fulfill your purpose and achieve those hidden dreams waiting to be fulfilled.

I know you are eager to begin, but before we do, let's get started with the following prayer before moving on to the next chapter —Words of Encouragement.

Father, I thank You for each of Your sons and daughters that You have led to read this book. Even if they do not know that is who they are, or yet feel it in their hearts, it is still Your divine plan that they be here and I personally thank You for their obedience to follow the leading of Holy Spirit. Your word says that You will enlighten the eyes of our understanding and you will give it freely to those who ask. So I thank You that they will gain the great revelation and spiritual nuggets contained in the pages of this book that will produce the understanding that You desire them to have. Father, encourage their hearts to be assured that You will never leave them nor forsake them. I pray that they will humbly submit themselves to You to be used to reveal Your glory in the earth. Father, I bind the hand of the enemy that will try to cause them to miss out on the blessing You have waiting for them to receive here. Let not one word that You have for them fall to the ground, but let them receive the rich and abundant harvest You have planned for them. I release a fresh new anointing to destroy every yoke of bondage in Jesus name. Amen.

CHAPTER ONE

Words of Encouragement

Welcome! You have just taken the first step through the door of a brand new experience that has been waiting for you to arrive. God is already starting to reveal part of His portrait for the next phase of your life.

There will be many challenges and discoveries to assist you in uncovering the true you and preparing you to be who He desires you to be in this season of your life. You will be stretched beyond your wildest imagination. I guarantee the reward will be well worth it when you have finished through the process of His plan.

Every day is going to be an adventure with the lover of your soul. Through the leading of Holy Spirit, you will start to see His hand orchestrating in everything. Know that you are being prepared to move in places you have never been before and to do things that you never thought you would do.

In this phase of the process you must rely on His gift of faith and trust Him to cultivate that which has already been planted deep inside you. It may sound risky or hard to believe, but trust the plans that He has for you according to Jeremiah 29:11.

If you embrace the journey as the biggest classroom of life and strive to be a student who excels, you will do well. The knowledge that will be released will build a firm foundation for you to continue to soar higher in your purpose and display your uniqueness. Nothing will be denied to you as you move forward in the Master's plan.

You are the only person that can limit the possibilities that await you. Nothing is more fulfilling and enriching than to see your passion to obey Him and help others in the process of accomplishing their goals. You were created for a purpose and on purpose by the greatest mastermind to ever exist.

You are not an accident, but you are a thought and a manifestation directly from the very heart of God. You were created to be used by the mighty hand of God to bring Him worship, glory, and honor. You have the power to change atmospheres, influence people, and deliver souls from out of darkness.

I challenge you to wake up every morning excited about impossibilities being turned into possibilities through exercising your faith and standing firm on the truth of God's Word. There is a shift in momentum that will make you want to step out in a realm of faith and trust in Him unlike anything you have ever experienced before this point. I don't claim to know what is going on inside of you, but I know that He is stirring up and reviving you to fulfill your divine purpose because of your choice to read this book.

Remember to do your best through obeying His commands. Spend time in His presence so that you can know His voice as a loved sheep if you are not already doing so. You can only be classified as a failure if you never try to do what He commands of you. He will give you the strength and the ability to do great exploits in His kingdom.

"Therefore I say unto you, What things soever ye desire, when ye

pray, believe that ye receive them, and ye shall have them" — Mark 11:24.

Yes, there are and will be many negative or critical voices on the inside and outside of you, but you have to push past all of that and keep your target in clear focus. Each day you must take steps by opening up to His leading which will help you become one step closer to being successful in completing your goals and maturing His seed of purpose in you.

You see fulfilling purpose is a progressive thing, but the journey will always lead to another more fulfilling opportunity to arrive at the expected end of God's plan for you. Keeping an open mind is crucial and critical to the fulfillment of your divinely inspired purpose. Proverbs 3:5-6 states, *"Trust in the Lord with all thine heart; and lean not to thine own understanding. In all thy ways acknowledge him, and he shall direct thy paths."* It is simply a matter of wholeheartedly trusting and having full confidence in God.

Now it is time to take a deep breath and take action by turning the page to learn how unforgiveness can rob you of God's blessings and your life of purpose. Best wishes and remember there will be times when you have to encourage yourself just like King David.

"And David was greatly distressed: for the people spake of stoning him, because the soul of all the people was grieved, every man for his sons and for his daughters but David encouraged himself in the LORD his God" — 1 Samuel 30:6.

Everything you need is only a prayer and praise away.

CHAPTER TWO

Unforgiveness

The seed of unforgiveness forms when we are rejected, abandoned, and betrayed if we don't quickly forgive. Over a period of time strongholds develop which give the enemy a legal right to attack us. Unforgiveness opens the door for spirts of bitterness, anger, jealousy, perfectionism, suspicion, fear, etc.

In Matthew 6:14-15, we are told in order to be forgiven we must forgive. It is just that simple. For Christians, forgiveness is a major part of our beliefs. Without the ability to forgive, we cannot be forgiven by the Father.

Peter asked Jesus if he should forgive his brother who sinned against him up to seven times. Perhaps you may be surprised like Peter was at Jesus' response. "*Jesus saith unto him, I say not unto thee, Until seven times; but, Until seventy times seven*" (Matthew 18:21-22). We are commanded to forgive four hundred ninety times whether we are asked to or not. Can you see now how important forgiveness is to the Father?

Unforgiveness in any form blocks the way to reaching our full potential. It cuts to the very core of our innermost being. It hinders us from truly seeing ourselves as God sees us.

I have forgiven many of the people who have hurt me in my life, but I never truly allowed God to deal with the painful memories connected to my experiences. God not only forgives us of our sins, but He also forgets them.

"And their sins and iniquities will I remember no more" — Hebrews 10:17.

He does not require more of us than He is willing to do for us and through us. Rely on Him to help you forgive those who have hurt you in anyway. Let's look at the story of the unforgiving servant.

Matthew 18:23-35 talks about a servant who owed the king a great deal of money that he was unable to repay. He pleaded with the king to have mercy on him. The king had compassion and cancelled the entire debt. As this servant left the king's presence, he saw another servant who owed him much less money than what he had owed the king.

The second servant pleaded for mercy telling him how he could not repay the debt. The first servant was merciless and demanded full payment. In his anger, he had the second servant thrown in jail.

Observers who witnessed what had transpired between the two servants reported back to the king. The first servant was brought before the king who severely reprimanded him. Because of the servant's unforgiveness, he was imprisoned and turned over to the hands of the tormentors for punishment.

This illustration shows that unforgiveness opens the door for attack from the enemy in the form of a spirit of torment. The spirit of torment becomes your prison guard ensuring that you stay in the grips of bondage until you repent and forgive. This spirit is a hard task master, because it keeps replaying the scene over in your head and the feelings grow stronger.

You lose valuable time and the quality of your life is greatly diminished. You become separated from God and unable to fulfill your purpose. We are told in Isaiah 61:1 that God binds up the brokenhearted. Your part is to give it to Him by desiring to forgive the person and let God replace the hurt with love.

The spirit of unforgiveness can masquerade as mistrust, jealousy, and suspicion in our relationships. There is a tendency to judge others by our past experiences associated with our deep feelings of hurt. This mindset limits us from truly experiencing joy and forming healthy relationships.

I know that it is human nature to judge according to past experiences—especially when strongholds have been deeply rooted and established in us. We are instructed not to judge according to appearance, but to judge righteously based on the word of God (John 7:24).

I discovered that I hadn't forgiven myself for my role in allowing myself to be hurt, used, and abused by those who I truly loved and wanted to help. I forgave on the surface, but I was still holding anger, bitterness, and other negative feelings in my heart. The scars were very deep because of years of abuse. Perhaps, you too can relate to such pain?

By holding on to that inner hurt, I stayed depressed, suspicious, and very untrusting of people, and even God for allowing these things to occur in my life. I developed a sabotage spirit, which sabotaged every relationship before it got too close. I always made sure that I had an out and that I would only let my feelings get so far.

Once I reached the point of my planned exit door, I would use any excuse I could find to end the relationship. The irony was by that point it was already too close, when I started feeling threatened by it. I would spend days depressed and hurt because I knew I had ruined a good relationship.

Time helped me to partially heal, but I stayed stuck in this endless cycle, until I started to fulfill the true purpose on my life. I haven't mastered it one hundred percent yet, but I am much better at recognizing the signs and fighting against it. I have learned to turn it over to God and apply the truth of His word to my thought life.

God's Word explains the true attributes of unconditional love in 1 Corinthians 13:4-8a. I especially like verse 7 that says, *"Beareth all things, believeth all things, hopeth all things, and endureth all things."* This is God's love for us and it is the love that we are to have for each other.

Another thing that I have learned is that apart from the assistance of the Holy Spirit, I am incapable of truly forgiving anyone. It is through His power that I can forgive—even when a person doesn't ask. By God's love, I am able to pray for Him to abundantly bless those who have truly traumatized my life.

The flesh always wants to be in control and protect itself from any type of pain or change. You may be saying to yourself that this is a good thing, right? To some degree you are correct. God has a plan for our lives that is beyond just us.

Seeds of forgiveness produce great continual harvests of good fruit when they are cared for properly. Unforgiveness causes crops to produce minimal results and rotten fruit. God knows the right mixture of manure, sunlight, and rain. Notice I started with manure. Manure or fertilizer is the substance that helps things grow and mature. God will cause your seeds of forgiveness to grow.

As it is with plants, so is it with us. In the process of growth, we are going to encounter those that will hurt us, but we cannot let that stop us from doing what is right according to His word and will for our lives. Know that these things are necessary to produce the fruit of righteousness in you and to plant seeds in those who you are able to influence with your lifestyle.

Our mindset has to be that of forgiveness no matter what. We do this so that we can keep the channels open. Forgiveness also allow us to stay under God's protective covering.

Here is a truth for you to think about. In the moment when we hurt someone else in our lifetimes—whether willingly or unknowingly—we are the reflection of those who have hurt us in the past. This is why forgiveness is so important and crucial to our well-being and the well-being of others, so that our hurts and bitterness do not come to harm others.

God's Word describes the nature of our hearts and His thoughts about it in Jeremiah 17:9-10, *"The heart is deceitful above all things, and desperately wicked: who can know it? I the Lord search the heart, I try the reins, even to give every man according to his ways, and according to the fruit of his doings."*

The word describes the heart as deceitful and desperately wicked and that is why the enemy can easily utilize it to his advantage through an unforgiving spirit. It is better to walk and stand on the truth of God's Word which takes away Satan's ability to attack us.

I am rediscovering myself by paying close attention to how I react to situations that hurt or make me angry. Now I take the time to analyze the situation to determine the root cause of why I reacted the way I did. I then pray and ask the Holy Spirit to remove the root or place where the enemy can gain access to attack.

I am on the road to recovery by allowing God to go into the hidden places of my heart and deal with the deep-seated hurt and soul wounds that have not been dealt with. He is bringing forth His healing for both my past and present hurts and wounds.

In order to love like He does, He desires for us to be more vulnerable, open, and honest to discuss our hurts even in times when we are misunderstood or taken for granted. I do this so I am able to continue moving in the things I am purposed to do. Realizing this has helped me to keep moving forward to excel in my service to God, I strive every day to mature in developing the nature and character of Jesus Christ. It is His example that we are called to follow and emulate so others can experience His love and be drawn unto Him.

Take action to move forward in fulfilling your purpose, because what you carry on the inside of you is vitally important for the rest of us on this planet. Otherwise, you would not have been given the opportune privilege to be sent here for such a time as this.

Many are waiting on that precious seed that grows inside of you. Remember, you were led to read this book that I was led to write. Don't waste another second. Open up the prison doors and free all the prisoners including yourself. I dare you to let go, give all the pain to God and walk in the rest He has for you by totally trusting Him.

By choosing to forgive yourself and others, you disarm the power of the enemy to strip you of your birthright and kingly inheritance. Forgiveness allows the promised seed of purpose given by the Father to contribute to your sphere of influence and to the betterment of the earth as a whole. Let it go and let God free you from the bondages that so easily beset you.

It is time to shut the door on past hurts stemming from childhood, adulthood, and life's circumstances. If you haven't taken the time to give these hurts to the Lord and ask for forgiveness, please stop and take time to do so before moving on to the next chapter.

God is waiting for you to come and be alone with Him in His presence.

CHAPTER THREE

Alone in His Presence

This is probably my favorite chapter of this book to write, because it is one of my most favorite things to do. I am a worshipper. I am a woman after God's own heart. I relentlessly chase after Him.

Walking on this road of purpose can sometimes be lonely, but it is in the solitude when you develop a greater sense of your purpose and who you are in Him. You start to see many valuable nuggets of the seed inside you starting to break the ground of fulfillment. It takes being alone to come face to face with the person who is truly the being that He created for His pleasure.

Understand that we are vital and valuable to add to the inherent value of those we encounter on this journey of purpose. The lesson is that we must share what the Holy Spirit is leading us to do or say whether it is received or not. See, when you share yourself with others, seeds are being planted that will grow long after you have moved on.

We all possess the ability to put an indelible mark in the earth through what we share. Books, conversations, and everyday experiences all have the ability to influence our thoughts which aid in creating our worlds and our responses. It is amazing the variety of things that mold and shape us as individuals that we are totally unaware of.

One of my favorite Scriptures is Proverbs 4:23 where we are told to guard our hearts for out of it flows the issues of life. The heart in this instance is our minds, because out of our minds flows the thoughts that shape the life we live. We must be extremely careful who we give the power to influence our thought life.

People of purpose know how to tap into the true source of power. This ensures that their pathways will stay straight and that they will be able to keep moving forward in difficult times of testing. The testing is sent to reveal many of the character flaws that need to be weeded out and replaced by more of His light of truth in us.

Psalm 91 talks about dwelling in the secret place of the most High and dwelling under the shadow of the Almighty. This is the place where the Great Shepherd leads us beside the still waters and give us green pastures to lie down in sweet rest with Him (Psalm 23).

Being alone in His presence brings the necessary refreshment, revitalization, and restoration to moving forward in walking out our purpose. This is a place where we get further instructions. In His presence is such a peace that calms all of our fears and gives us the ability to hear His still small voice.

I love being in this place, because it gives me an assurance that He will never leave me nor forsake me when the storms of life come (Hebrews 13:5). It is not only the fact that we have the opportunity to enjoy His companionship, but we get to develop a deep, intimate relationship with Him. In this place we are surrounded by His love for us. He longs for us to come to this place to commune and sup with Him, but many are too busy or place things above Him to spend time with Him in His secret place.

People of purpose know that their very existence depends on being with Him. He is the Creator of all things good and bad. He knows and ordained everything that we are purposed to do even before He created the world. Do you go and commune with Him on a daily basis to discover His heart for you? If not, I exhort you to make this a priority as you continue to uncover your purpose and until you take your final breath on this earth.

As often as you can be alone in His presence, you are guaranteed to find a peaceful rest. This place, if entered into correctly, has a soothing effect on a tired and weary soul. There is a time of preparation before one can enter into the secret place because it is the sacred and holy dwelling place of Almighty God.

Psalm 100:4 tells us how to begin to enter into this place. We are to come before Him with thanksgiving, praise, and blessing His Holy name. There is nothing more beautiful to God than a thankful and grateful heart filled to capacity in obedience to Him.

"The Lord thy God in the midst of thee is mighty: he will save, he will rejoice over thee with joy; he will rest in his love, he will joy over thee with singing" Zephaniah — 3:17.

From Zephaniah we see what occurs when God is happy:

- His might is displayed
- Salvation is evident
- He rejoices over us with His joy which strengthens us
- There is a rest in His love
- He sings because we have made Him happy

This is the place that I look forward to reaching on a daily basis. My goal is to please and make the Lord sing every day. I want His heart to be overjoyed because I have brought my gifts of praise and worship instead of constantly petitioning Him to do things in my life.

Although, sometimes it may seem like God doesn't care or has totally forgotten us, we can rest assured that is not the case. He truly cares about us like a faithful Father even in the midst of our times of disobedience and independence.

Being alone with Him and discovering His heart is the true connection needed to fulfilling your purpose and using your talents, gifts, and resources. This should always be our starting point every day and not just in times when the way seems uncertain.

In this place we chase after His heart like David—the one who was labeled a man after God's own heart (Acts 13:22). Nothing pleases God more than for His children to spend time seeking His heart on the things that matter to them. If it is important to you, it is important to God.

I am still learning how not to come into His presence without my preconceived notions for the answers I seek. I am grateful He is always patient and long suffering in the times when I just have to do it my way. It doesn't take as long now for me to come around to His way of thinking.

Learning to allow Him to mold and shape my thoughts, ways, and plans is essentially gained from the time I spend alone with Him on a daily basis. I am able to do it more now that I have retired, but I encourage you to make the sacrifice if you work. When I would sacrifice that extra hour or half hour in the morning, my days ran much smoother than when I was rushed out of the house without doing it.

Apostle Daryl Davis taught me how to spend time in God's presence when we would have all night prayer sessions at our church. We would spend six hours two nights a week for almost two years, praying, praising, and worshiping God. I grew immensely during these times. In the end of Hebrew 11:6, I learned that God rewards those who diligently seek Him. What I found out during these times of all night prayer was that He was the reward. There is no greater places to be than in His presence and in His word.

He also taught me to work my way up to spending at least three hours a day worshiping and praising the Lord. He said that by doing this "we would retire from worrying." I must admit, Apostle Daryl was absolutely right. Now when I start to feel worry coming on, I immediately start to praise God and soon that spirit lifts. Apostle Daryl instructed us that praise sets an ambush for the enemy. If you are being attacked, start praising God (2 Chronicles 20:22). The words say that God inhabits the praise of His people (Psalm 22:3). Where the Spirit of the Lord is there is liberty (2 Corinthians 3:17). Praise is a powerful weapon in the hands of a believer.

Man was not created to be independent or separate from God's intervention. God created us to have a relationship with Him. He desires to lovingly provide for our well-being and all of our needs. He knows we need these times of refreshing to just be able to deal with life and the things that come with it.

My hope is that as you read through this chapter that you now desire more intimacy with the lover of your soul and the creator of your being. He desires to have all of you to Himself.

He is a jealous God who is so much in love with you. He loves the very essence of your presence just like you enjoy His when He draws near to you. He gave His only begotten Son that you would have life and have it more abundantly (John 3:16, 10:10b).

Before we move to the next chapter, please take a moment to reflect on your relationship and the time you spend in God's presence. I pray that you are making plans to spend more time to go deeper and come up higher in Him.

CHAPTER FOUR

Overcoming Fear

Why is it important to overcome fear? A spirit of fear can rob you of your purpose. Overcoming fear is the next stage in your journey to discovering your purpose.

The number one weapon the enemy uses to interfere with God's plans is fear. It is a paralyzing spirit sent to abort and destroy the seed of purpose from coming into full maturation. It is designed to hinder forward motion through its paralyzing effect. Many times when faced with change, an overwhelming sense of fear comes over us.

We waste so much time battling fear. Many times the things we make up in our minds never happen. Again fear is a time waster that should not be entertained. If anything, let your fear empower you to push forward into the unknown territory of possibilities waiting for you.

Fear does not come from God, but is in direct correlation with the kingdom of darkness. "*God did not give us a spirit of fear, but of power, love, and a sound mind*" (1 Timothy 1:7). Fear, as I mentioned in the chapter on unforgiveness, can enter in from being rejected, abandoned, betrayed, deeply hurt, or through traumatic experiences. After we have experienced any of these things, fear finds a place to hide and control us by constantly bringing back the memories and the attached emotions.

Have you ever asked yourself these questions: "What am I actually afraid of when it comes to fulfilling my purpose?" "Why am I afraid to do what I know deep in my heart I was created to do?" I have asked myself these same questions many times when facing change and doing something different. We have to push past the feeling of fear and do what we are instructed to do.

One of the things that I had to overcome was the fear of people's opinions and always trying to please them. I was afraid of not being liked or being alone. The major reason I placed a high value on being liked was because of the rejection I have suffered as a child.

Being heavier and taller than most of my friends, they always made fun of me and even physically tried to abuse me. I wasn't a fighter and even to this day, I stay away from chaos and confusion. When I am walking in the power of Holy Spirit, none of those things matter. I like things to be peaceful, calm, and comfortable, but God seemed to always have a different plan for my life.

"There is no fear in love; but perfect love caseth out fear, because fear hath torment. He that feareth is not made perfect in love" — 1 John 4:18.

Perfect love is a very powerful tool that overcomes fear. The only place we can find perfect love is in the presence of our perfect God. The Father has graciously given us power, love, and a sound mind to overcome such an opposing enemy.

This chapter was written to help you overcome fear, which can prevent you from fulfilling your purpose and achieving your dreams. By laying the proper foundation on God's words of truth, you will be able to condition your mind to guard against the enemy's attacks.

By becoming aware of when the debilitating spirit of fear may begin to overwhelm you, seek out the truth of God's Word and pray for His strength to be victorious every time. Here are a couple of powerful Scriptures you can memorize and say when fear tries to attack you.

"Nay, in all these things we are more than conquerors through him that loved us" — Romans 8:37.

"I can do all things through Christ which strengtheneth me" — Philippians 4:13.

Some additional reference sources for finding Scriptures on fear are:

- The concordance in the back of your Bible
- The online version of the Strong's Concordance on the Internet
- Google search (Scriptures on fear)

Before moving on to the next chapter, please take a moment to get still and think about any fear you are currently dealing with. Write it down on a sheet of paper and then eliminate it with God's Word and taking time to pray.

CHAPTER FIVE

Eliminating Negative Influences and Opinions

Do opinions from others really matter? Depending upon who they come from, they can carry a great deal of weight in our decision making process.

I wrote this chapter to shed clarity on an area I struggled with for a great number of years. I allowed people's opinions to become my reality about myself in many instances. Opinions contributed to my self-image and self-esteem.

Every day we are inundated with the opinions, advice, and criticisms of others. The opinions and perceptions we form about ourselves are often based on what others say about or to us. Many opinions are formulated based on limited information. We must remember they are just that—opinions. They may contain some truth, but that is not always the case.

God has given us the ability to choose what we allow to enter into our minds. It is through our thoughts that we are equipped to shape our lives and walk out our divine purpose. Our thoughts lead us to the choices we make which direct our lives.

They can be empowering or deflating. Believing the false or negative opinions of others can be a detriment to our thoughts.

Opinions can be very misleading and they can stop your ability to excel if they come from a trusted friend or reliable source. I think Shakespeare said it best, *"to thine ownself be true"*. It is very hard to do this when you do not know who you are and what you are capable of doing.

If you are honest as you continue this journey, you will see some characteristics and personality flaws exposed that are not so pretty. But as we continue to expose them to the light of the truth of His word, they will be changed over time to become a good part of us—if you have the fortitude. In this instance it should be your ultimate goal to know what you are up against.

Fulfilling your purposes will show you just what you are made of and what is true about you. It is the consuming fire of God that brings forth the pure gold residing on the inside of you.

People of purpose know that they will never obtain success and fulfill their purpose by listening to negative beliefs and opinions of others. Those whose opinions we value may mean well, but they can stop the plan of God for our lives. Even when we are attempting the same thing that someone else may have struggled with, the outcome can be totally different based on our approach to and experience with the situation. This is especially true if what we are attempting is not part of God's plan for our life.

Look at the first generation of the Israelites. They didn't see the Promised Land because they believed in the negative reports of the ten spies who said there were giants in the land. They did not trust God to be able to fulfill His promise of bringing them into the land flowing with milk and honey (Numbers 13 and Deuteronomy 1).

Opinions can be deemed good or bad based on our experiences

and our level of self-esteem and self-image we possess at any time. No matter what is said, it does not have to be permanent or have a permanent effect on our lives. We as people of purpose possess the ability to move out of the realm of opinion and human limitations and into the realm of fulfillment and successful outcomes.

Every day we are presented with changes and challenges. It is crucial on this journey to guard against people's opinions and stand on the truth of God's Word. For He is the author and finisher of our faith and the one who provides everything for the completion of the journey (Hebrews 12:2).

Thoughts have the ability to produce fruit that will manifest in your life. Look at the fruit that the thought bears in your mind. Do the thoughts produce a desire to grow in a positive way? Do they give you energy to press harder and move forward along the path God has set before you? If not, then weigh them very carefully before taking heed to them. The word of God in 2 Corinthians 10:6 instructs us to, *"cast down imaginations, and every high thing that exalt itself against the knowledge of God, and bring into captivity every thought to the obedience of Christ."*

Many times we get used to living by standards others have set for us by allowing them to become our true way of life. When this happens, then roots of bitterness, insecurity, and feeling unappreciated will develop.

I found that being a people pleaser I was trying to fill a need through being needed and in control. I was often taken advantage of or neglected with many of my needs unfulfilled. I would become angry at myself for falling into this trap, but would not take the necessary actions to break this cycle in my life. I truly didn't value or love myself because I didn't feel I was worthy of being loved.

The interesting thing about low self-esteem is that it can affect anyone. It is based on how a person views and values himself or herself. It is reflective in what we allow ourselves to believe based on what others say about us and how they treat us for the sake of keeping the relationship.

I remember meeting a very beautiful young lady at a recent conference I attended. As we talked, I recognized she had very low self-esteem. As I sat listening to her, I thought she was breathtakingly beautiful with a good heart, but she didn't see herself as being beautiful at all. This helped me to see that low self-esteem is not based on an outward appearance per se, but it stems from inner turmoil from the person's thought life.

It was so ironic that we shared similar traits and experienced many of the same things. We both longed for men to love us, but ended up in very toxic and devastating relationships. I also discovered from our conversation that fear was stopping us both from saying no more and moving on to something better.

I am including the part about self-esteem and self-image to this book because it can hinder the fulfillment of your purpose. When we become distracted by the pressures of fitting in and feeling inadequate, then that can sometimes stop the flow of what you need to move forward in God's plan for your life.

"In all things we are more than conquerors through him that loved us" —Romans 8:37.

Now that I have learned to let go of toxic relationships, I am exhilarated by the power of saying no. Finally, I believe that I am a conqueror and have accepted the fact that it is perfectly okay if people choose to be displeased by what I do or don't do that differs from what they wanted. I made up my mind that God was the only one I was devoted to pleasing.

It takes practice every time the challenges appear, but through consistency it will become a lasting fix. You will finally be in better control of you, which gives you more power and the ability to be who you are created to be. It is time to come back into alignment with the thoughts and plans that God has for you.

We have come to the end of the road on eliminating negative influences and opinions. Please take a moment to reflect on your life.

Are there any areas you can see based on negative opinions and influences that you need to address? If so, please take the time you need before moving on to the next chapter called Old Things Pass Away.

CHAPTER SIX

Old Things Pass Away

My goal in this chapter is to teach you how to recognize and eliminate the thoughts that affect mindsets, habits, feelings, relationships, and lifestyles and to assist you in fulfilling your purpose.

Each of us have a side that we especially don't like or care for. I call mine the dark side. I try to keep her locked up and constantly tell people when I feel her trying to surface, "that you really don't want to mess with the lock to her cage because it is not going to be nice."

Recently, I was speaking with my sister concerning this and God informed me that He created me whole and not to be separated from this part of me. He told me that she also needs to be loved. He created her to be nurtured and to be one with me to strengthen and give me balance.

Too many of us are walking around fragmented in the natural sense because of things we have suffered through our lives. I get it, but it still does not change the fact that God created each of us to be a whole person who He loves unconditionally. He didn't send Jesus here to redeem only the good part of us, He came here to redeem us completely.

God desires to show us how to develop balance and how to love that part that we feel is unlovable. Psalm 139:13-17 (CEV) says:

You are the one who put me together inside my mother's body, and I praise you because of the wonderful way you created me. Everything you do is marvelous! Of this I have no doubt. Nothing about me is hidden from you! I was secretly woven together deep in the earth below, but with your own eyes you saw my body being formed. Even before I was born, you had written in your book everything I would do. Your thoughts are far beyond my understanding, much more than I could ever imagine.

This Scripture tells us that God put us together and placed us in our mother's womb according to the design He thought up for each of us. He knew exactly everything that would happen in our life, every character flaw we would experience, and the good and bad that we would do. He made provision for each of us through the redemptive power of the cross.

These dark personality traits must be constantly exposed to the light of truth when they surface so that they can be brought under the rulership and sovereignty of the Lord Jesus Christ. He is the one who makes us whole and able to function according to His will.

God's Word states in 2 Corinthians 5:17, "*Therefore if any man be in Christ, he is a new creature: old things are passed away; behold, all things are become new.*" It is the blood of Jesus Christ and His saving grace that makes us whole and new.

Everything starts in the mind and from there proceeds to formulate thought patterns. Thoughts and words are two very powerful elements in our human structure. They are significant in determining the level to which we succeed or fail. Our experiences shape our thoughts which ultimately shape our lives.

When these thoughts first entered in, we think on them and then they begin to form into mental pictures that convert into actions and habits. We classify habits as either good or bad, mainly based on our perception of them.

In my formable years, I was never taught the true importance of the power of thoughts or words. Proverbs 23:7 says, *"For as he thinketh in his heart, so is he:"* Romans 12:2 tells us to *"be not conformed to this world: but be ye transformed by the renewing of your mind."* This takes place by meditating on the word of God.

We are so inundated with the stress and pressure in our daily lives that it becomes a sweet haven of rest to be able to discard these thoughts in exchange for peaceful ones. Isaiah 26:3 states that we will be kept in perfect peace if our minds our stayed on God.

Thoughts are so important to God that He recorded the blueprint for our thoughts in His word. He instructs us to think on things that are true, honest, just, pure, lovely, and of a good report (Philippians 4:8). We must filter every thought and bring it under the obedience of Jesus Christ (2 Corinthians 10:5). This is to keep the seed of purpose in us safe from those that seek to destroy it from benefitting others.

If you examine your life right now, you will see what your thoughts have produced. Listening to our conversations that we have with ourselves and with others on a daily basis will reveal the core essence of our thoughts. What you may find is a lot of negative thoughts and conversations are being exchanged and acted upon by the atmosphere to bring them into existence.

It is imperative that we watch over every thought and only allow those that are conducive to bring forth the light of truth to nurture and develop our seeds of purpose. We have been given a tremendous opportunity to be used by God to invoke change in our minds, homes, families, jobs, communities, cities, and other places human relationships occur.

I hope that what you have experienced thus far in this book has begun to change how you think and perceive things. God is about building up the body of believers and increasing the inhabitants of His kingdom. The seed of purpose you carry will do just that as you release your old thinking patterns and allow Him to renew your mind to come into alignment with His.

He tells us in His word that we need to aspire to come up higher in our thinking.

"For my thoughts are not your thoughts, neither are your ways my ways, saith the Lord. For as the heavens are higher than the earth, so are my ways higher than your ways, and my thoughts than your thoughts" — Isaiah 55:8-9.

Are you ready to embark on letting go of the former things and thought patterns to ascend higher into the realm of God-like thoughts? He is standing by to assist and strengthen you as you fulfill your divine purpose. In order to assist you in this process, I am going to ask you to complete these following steps before moving on to the next chapter.

Find a quiet place. Please get a sheet of paper, a pen, and a timer. Prepare to set the timer for ten minutes.

1. Once the timer starts, write down every thought that comes to your mind without changing it in any way. When the timer is up, review the thoughts you wrote down.

As you review your list what do you notice about what you wrote? Are your responses more negative than positive?

2. If you notice that the majority were mainly negative thoughts, I am going to ask you to commit for at least the next ten days to pay attention to every one of your thoughts. If it is negative, discard it quickly and replace it with a positive thought,

affirmation to speak to the opposite of the thought, or a Scripture. (Although I suggested ten days, twenty-one days would be better to form a new habit).

By completing this exercise you will start to stand guard over your thoughts and you will become more disciplined over your thoughts.

Remember, thoughts come with an attached destination. You have been given the power for the itinerary in which they will follow in your life. The next stop on your journey of purpose is learning how to believe in your true self.

Let's turn the page when you are ready to move forward in discovering what God has waiting for you in the next chapter.

CHAPTER SEVEN

Believing in Your True Self

Belief and faith builds up our trust in God which is necessary to embark upon and complete our journey of purpose. Without possessing these two superpowers it becomes impossible to believe and receive God's promises for the fulfillment of His plan for our lives. Another one of my favorite Scriptures is found in Hebrews 11:6, *"But without faith it is impossible to please him: for he that cometh to God must believe that he is, and that he is a rewarder of them that diligently seek him."*

If we do not believe that He is who He says He is, then it is impossible to please or receive from Him. The Gospel of Mark 11:24 declares, *"Therefore I say unto you, What things so ever ye desire, when ye pray, believe that ye receive them, and ye shall have them."* In order to receive, the key is to believe without any doubt during the time we wait on Him to release the answers.

Doubt and unbelief are two weapons the enemy uses to destroy our faith in God. I think that if God moved on my timetable these would not be an issue. These things simply come to test and strengthen our faith.

The Scriptures constantly reiterate that we must believe and have faith. Christianity is founded on love, but for me truth and faith also strengthens my foundation to trust completely in Him. Paul talks about the shield of faith that dispels the fiery darts of the enemy (Ephesians 6:16). This shield protects us from the attacks of the enemy, because it destroys the belief in the lies he uses to sway us from truly trusting God.

It is very important that we know our belief systems start inside of us and then manifests to the outer or natural realm. James instructs us that a double-minded man is unstable in all of his ways and let not that man think he will receive anything from God (1:7). Instability is the evidence of not fully trusting or believing that God is all He says He is and can do all that He promises to do from His word.

I am laying the foundation from the spiritual realm first so that you will be better equipped to deal with the flesh or carnal nature. You need to know how to effectively stand guard as you move forward in your purpose. The enemy always knows our weak areas to execute his attacks.

My brother taught me to move the sore spot so that when the enemy comes there would be no reaction to allow disturbance to my peace. Developing a healthy, Scripture-based belief system is essential to fulfilling dreams and walking in purpose. The more positive-oriented we are, the more creative and capable of receiving all that God has purposed for us as His children we will be.

God has given us the power of the spoken word that creates life and death. Strict attention should be placed on guarding what is heard and spoken. Words are a great influencer on creative matter as noted in the first chapter when God spoke and it manifested.

People of purpose skillfully select their words to saturate the atmosphere and everything that is connected to their lives. They begin and end each day with words that are energetic, encouraging, positive, and uplifting. They are normally avid readers of Scriptures and self-help books that help them stay centered and positive.

I am very sensitive to the Spirit and I tend to have to fight off spirits of depression and negative emotions. I do this by reading and speaking the word, listening to praise and worship music, or I just start laughing until I am back on a more positive plane. The key is to get the focus back on God and less on me and the issues I am facing at the time.

Walking the road of purpose takes knowing and believing who we are in Christ and who He is in us. It is easy to be thrown off track when we are unsure of who we are and the power that we possess. Greater is he that is in us than he that is in the world (1 John 4:4). We have power over all the works of the enemy and nothing by any means should harms us (Luke 10:19).

I have spent plenty of time beating myself up, because I did not look at life as a journey of lessons to be learned. I've always strived to be perfect, but that put a major strain on my belief system causing me to be controlling and overly frustrated. I know you are probably saying to yourself, didn't she know she wasn't perfect from the beginning? To answer that question, yes I did, but it still didn't stop me from trying. Perfectionism stems from a spirit of pride, in which God is constantly humbling me.

If you keep hitting a wall with your head, you will eventually discover that it hurts and does great damage. Sometimes, it takes a little longer for the light of understanding to take effect until we start to see it God's way. God does have a way to bring us around to His point of view.

Doing the same thing over and over again only produces the same results unless the plan is revisited and a new process is established. Countless hours of wasted energy, potential, and time is the outcome of trying to work it out based on what we know and see. The high road is to go to the Father first and follow the instructions He gives us.

From the early stages of childhood, our environment and associates formulate our belief patterns based on what we see and receive. We tend to gravitate to that which we have knowledge of thereby forming the path we venture down in life. These patterns are changed based on new experiences that ignite that inner spark of God's prompting to move to the next step of our purpose.

No matter what there has to be a level of courage and encouragement to pursue that inner voice that desires to do what the person is passionate about. Most of the time the safe zone is achieved because of the low tolerance for risk, failure, and rejection. To believe in yourself, you must dare to express your uniqueness. We have to believe we are of great value, which is not being conceited, selfish, or thinking we are better than anyone else.

We all are here with a unique purpose from the Father's heart and mind. No one else is able to do what He has created you to do. Most of the time He is the only one who truly knows what that is, but He will share it with you when you complete the process of believing and trusting in His will.

Even if we have an introverted personality, there is something beautiful inside us that the world is waiting to experience or otherwise, you would not have been given the opportunity to be created by the Father and allowed to continue to live.

It is good to look at the glass as being half-full as opposed to it being half-empty. Find the silver cloud in every storm and know that no matter what is experienced in life, your core true self must be allowed to come forth. There are many waiting on you with all of your so-called character flaws and personality hiccups.

The seed of purpose that lies in you is the blessing for those that are allowed to connect with you on your journey of purpose. You must believe in the person God designed you to be.

Your assignment for this chapter, if you choose to accept it, is to gather as many Scriptures you can find on belief and faith found in the New Testament. Pick ten that you can start to use to assist you in building up your belief and faith muscles. Work with them daily until you have them committed to memory then add ten more until you reach the end of those that are listed in the word.

When you are ready to move on, turn the page to begin the Avoid Making Comparisons chapter. I guarantee you this will be an eye opener.

CHAPTER EIGHT

Avoid Making Comparisons

"Comparison is a work of Hell. It leads to 'envy'."

~ Lance Wallnau ~

We learned in the last chapter that you are unique and are not meant to be the same as anyone else. You need the gift and expression that God purposed to come through you. No matter who is similar or who may have similar thoughts as you, I want you to know that you and your voice matters.

Even as I started to write this book, you do not know how many books I came across expressing the same or similar thoughts concerning the fulfillment of purpose. Looking at all the ones out there, I started to doubt myself. I thought that I did not have anything of value to add to the subject matter. I want to encourage you like I had to encourage myself that what is in you matters and needs to be expressed.

We are valuable and what we have to say is valuable to be heard no matter what we may have been told in the past. We are the only one who can share our own personal experiences on any particular area. That makes you an expert on the subject of you.

What makes your perspective different is how you view it and live through it. Yes, it may share some common thread as that of other people, but there is that thread of uniqueness that only can be expressed by you. It is time to stop letting fear stifle your voice.

No one has exactly been through what you have been through because they do not possess your mind, heart, and the people involved in the experience. It can be similar in nature, but it will never be exactly the same. Expressing yourself adds value because it produces the platform for others to be able to learn and glean from your experiences through the sharing of your stories or testimonies.

It is so important to be yourself and not replicate someone else's experiences because you think their story is better or more exciting. This would totally go against God's plan for you. Press forward to discover your true self and let it be displayed for the whole world to see.

I am reminded of the Scripture that talks about the body and its functions. In 1 Corinthians 12:14-18 it says:

For the body is not one member, but many. If the foot shall say, Because I am not the hand, I am not of the body; is it therefore not of the body? And if the ear shall say, Because I am not the eye, I am not of the body; is it therefore not of the body? If the whole body were an eye, where were the hearing? If the whole were hearing, where were the smelling? But now hath God set the members every one of them in the body, as it hath pleased him.

This Scripture clarifies that we all have a specific function that is to be conveyed for the betterment of mankind from our unique spheres of influence which affect the world as a whole.

Comparing ourselves to those we deem successful or who we want to be like, tends to make us feel like we don't and can't measure up. This can be a very disheartening and destructive place for us to be. Each of us has unique talents, qualities, personalities, strengths, weaknesses, likes, and dislikes that God wants us to use for the fulfillment of our purpose.

There is a great deal of comparison that occurs among the saints in the majority of our churches. We see something that we like and we immediately start to want to covet it. It is time for us to start expressing that which is uniquely inside of us without fear of not measuring up or of feeling inadequate. You are important to the bigger picture of life.

Comparing ourselves, or what we are capable of accomplishing, is really a futile attempt to discover who we truly are. So many people fall into a low self-esteem and self-image because of the need to fit in and be validated. This pattern can be created in the beginning stages of our development stemming from the fact that we never truly understood our value.

The interesting thing about making comparisons is that it is very difficult to compare things that are not exactly alike. Even if they look the same on the surface, there is an inner difference. Each of us is fashioned to be a unique expression by the hands of God.

The only true comparison is found by lining up to the truth of the word of God. As we use this as our measuring tool, we will be keeping with the plan of the seed of purpose inside us. We will have the necessary food to keep it nourished and protected from the elements that try to snuff it out from reaching its full potential.

I hope that you have come to the realization that you are valuable and possess special attributes hand selected by God Himself. Those are the things that the Father loves to display when you allow Him to have full control. Seek Him daily for the revelation knowledge of your value and what He desires of you. Your ultimate purpose is to bring Him glory.

Take a moment to reflect on those who you may have been comparing yourself to.

What things do you see in them that intrigue you to desire to be like them? As you look at those qualities or things, is there any resemblance of them in yourself that may have not been cultivated yet to the level you see in them? If not the same quality, do you see a quality in you that is equally as good?

As you ponder on these questions ask Holy Spirit to help you find the value within yourself that can be better expressed with some work and practice.

The next chapter will also assist you in letting go of comparisons and embracing your unique self. Turn the page. Time to jump in with both feet. Surf's up!

CHAPTER NINE

Expressing Your Uniqueness

As I stated in the last chapter, there are no two things on the face of the earth that are exactly one hundred percent the same. Even identical twins differ in their thought process and appearance. It is just not readily evident to the naked eye. Nevertheless, God had a reason for them both being created from the same seed that split in the womb.

People of purpose pursue the will of God—not the will of man. There is something on the inside of you screaming to get out. Let those creative juices flow as you express your creativity to provide a solution to someone else's problem. You are a source to bring heaven to the earth through your very existence.

Looking out the window at the rain, I started to reflect on the uniqueness of each drop. I thought that a single rain drop has the ability to change whatever it touches. My next thought was that God created each drop to be different for a specific purpose with an expected end. Pondering on the uniqueness of raindrops, I came to the conclusion that God's original purpose for one thing enables another thing to occur. It is like a spark creating a fire that can turn into a blaze with the right elements in operation.

God ordains the time to send rain to release its purpose of producing the necessary water supply, cleansing the earth, adding water to streams and lakes, and moisturizing the plants and grass to grow. In the same way that God has a purpose and perfect timing for rain, He also has a plan for us to live out our purpose and be the positive influence. Unlike rain, we have the ability to fight against God's timing, but He always has a way of getting us back to His way of thinking.

Following the road to fulfilling our purpose, our thinking must line up with God's truth of who we are and what we are created to do. We are to look past the superficial to the true seed of uniqueness that resides within us. Revelation comes by spending time in the presence of the Creator. Sometimes we have to fight to embrace our uniqueness from those things that try to steal, kill, and destroy the seed of purpose within us. We are created for specific purposes and times of release. We each have a mission that no one else on this planet can fulfill.

All my life I wanted to fit in with what I called the "normal" people and to experience love and acceptance. It seems that everyone could find this place except me. It didn't matter where I went, I was never accepted, or so I thought.

You see my idea of fitting in came with having to conform to being like everyone else in the group. What I didn't understand was that I was on the outside looking in. I believe that there is a special art to blending your uniqueness where it looks like you are part of a group, but you really are just expressing who you are.

It took writing this book to gain that bit of revelation. Fitting in relates to finding your true place in the whole of life and not necessarily on an individual basis. Each of us are a piece inside the whole puzzle of life. We only fit in our proper place. If you force your piece to fit into a place that it doesn't belong it can ruin the place for other pieces to fit and connect to other pieces to complete the picture. It is crucial to let God put us in the proper place where we truly fit into His master plan.

Take a good long look in the mirror of your inner being and look at the things that make you unique. Take the time to examine what that seed is trying to express and pour it forth so others can be blessed. No matter how long it has been covered over with fear, doubts, or low self-esteem, it is bursting with life.

This seed has been hidden safely away in the darkness only getting brief sparks of light, water, and nourishment every time you had the faith to experience something new and come out of your comfort zone. We all like to stay in our nice, neat little compartments of complacency. Fortunately for us life happens to shake our worlds and push us forward to discover what really lies on the inside of us.

I have heard it is like peeling layers off until the core is exposed and there is no turning back, because there is nothing left to turn back to. We are tender plants in the Father's hands being fertilized by the manure of life, which is necessary to promote strong healthy growth. We grow and discover our true selves in the flames of the fires of adversity.

It is time to cultivate your uniqueness. You are a treasure in an earthen vessel waiting to be displayed for all the world around you to be touch by the fulfillment of your purpose. Dare to be you and not a clone of someone else.

Take comfort in knowing that you are not perfect and that it is ok to make mistakes along the way. Our character flaws and imperfections makes us the beautiful expression of uniqueness we were created to be. Do you realize that you are the very expression and masterpiece created by the mighty hand of God?

When God created you and placed you inside your mother's womb, He knew the exact recipe that made you who you would be at every stage of your life. He allows you to bake checking on you to see if you are ready to come out the oven. He inserts His knife into the center of your heart to ensure you come out clean. If you do not then, He places you back in the oven to continue to cook unto perfection. Constant testing and waiting in the oven of affliction is representative of what spiritual life is all about.

As we are allowed to cook in the Father's kitchen, He ensures that we sustain the proper bake time until we are that delicious bread of heaven that can be shared with the people of the earth to bring forth His bountiful blessings. We are His promised seed.

Each of us has a distinct role to advance the Kingdom of God. It is through our uniqueness and willingness to submit to His plan will we be able to fulfill our purpose. In Philippians 3:14, Paul reminded us, *"I press toward the mark for the prize of the high calling of God in Christ Jesus."* I know the road may be rough sometimes, but keep pressing forward like Paul did until you reach your expected end.

In this chapter we discovered the importance of being that unique expression that God created us to be. Maybe perhaps you are still struggling with really trying to find what is unique about you. Please take a moment to find a place where you can get still and quiet.

Your assignment is to close your eyes and just listen to your breathing patterns. You will do this until you sense a feeling of complete peace. Pray and ask the Father to reveal to you the unique things that He has put in you to be displayed for this time. Once He is done revealing it to you, write them down.

Now that you have discovered your unique things God has for you, it is time to move on to the next chapter called Gifts and Talents. This chapter will teach you about when things are used they bring forth multiplication. If you are ready, let's proceed to see what God desires to reveal to you by turning the page.

CHAPTER TEN

Gifts and Talents

> *"Every good gift and every perfect gift is from above, and cometh down from the Father of lights, with who is no variableness, neither shadow of turning"*
>
> — *James 1:17.*

You dear reader are that good and perfect gift given to the earth for such a time as this from the Father of lights, Almighty God. He strategically and faithfully put in you everything you will need to fulfill your purpose and assignment here on earth. What is inside of you is uniquely fashioned to fit you and to be shared with others to fulfill their divine purpose as well.

At the time of birth, we are endowed with certain gifts and talents that life tends to cultivate through our daily experiences. Take a minute and think back on your life from childhood to your adulthood. What things did you like doing that are still things that you enjoy doing today in your adult life? Have you ever noticed that you like some things and other things you don't? You tend to gravitate to certain things. These things that you gravitate to are your God given gifts and talents to be shared with the world.

For me, I liked things that were challenging and that I could do with my hands. I liked to sit and daydream a lot when I was a kid. I always strived to be the best and the fastest at whatever assignment we were given in school. Although I liked certain sports, I was not the athletic type. I always enjoyed writing and working with numbers. I won many writing contests growing up and I ended up getting a degree in Accounting and Finance to pursue my love for numbers.

When I was five, my mom taught me how to crochet. Then I ventured off to learning how to knit and latch hook. The only problem was I could not understand and follow the directions on the patterns, but I could look at the picture and make it look like what I saw.

Back in my twenties, I assembled all the buildings for the city we were constructing for my husband's model trains. The amazing part was most of the instructions were in German and I only speak English. God blessed me to be able to recreate things by what I saw and He gave me a photographic memory.

Talents are those things that lie inside of us that sometimes takes life and other people to help us discover. The funny thing about talent is that it comes in its raw form and then as we grow it grows with us. It rapidly grows with discovery and use.

We are all gifted with natural abilities to do certain things. You may not know what yours are yet, because perhaps you have never taken the time to stop and think about what they are or because they just come naturally for you and you just do them. In any event they are still there to be used.

I love the story of the talents founds in Matthew 25:14-30 about the nobleman who was traveling to a far country. He left talents with three servants. The first one he gave five talents, the second one he gave two, and the third one he gave one. Granted the talents in this Scripture is in reference to money, but the thought is still the same. With our gifts or natural abilities they are talents that can be used to produce money.

There is a purpose for having talents and a desired outcome with using them. As we read further in this Scripture, we see that the one with the five and the one with the two talents doubled their talents by using them. This reveals a great lesson on multiplication.

Let's stop a moment and see what is actually going on here. Those talents that we use will double with use. But without using them because of fear we lose the ability to multiply them. Are you still with me?

According to Genesis 1:28, God stated His purpose for Adam and Eve is to "*...be fruitful, and multiply, and replenish the earth and subdue it, and have dominion over. . . .*" Note one of the things they were created to do was multiply. This is an inherent gift that is part of our being as well.

What is the outcome for those that use their talents verses those who do not?

For the two servants who used their talents, their talents were doubled. The reward stated in Matthew 25:21, 23 says that they were called good and faithful, their rulership was increased, and they were given the privilege to enter into the joy of the Lord. These two servants received a greater outcome than what they could ever imagine because they were obedient to do something with what was entrusted for them to watch over.

Matthew 25:24-28 talks about the servant who was afraid. This servant was afraid of the nobleman because of his strict business success and certain strong characteristics. The servant immediately buried his gift in the earth to protect it from being lost.

The nobleman was greatly disappointed with the servant upon his returned. Not using his talent eliminated his chances to increase what he had. He was deemed a wicked, slothful, and unprofitable servant that did not bring forth value from using his given talent. Even in an extreme case he could have taken his talent to the bank and still made something from using it.

His talent was taken away and given to the one who now had ten talents. He was cast into outer darkness missing out on the great potential and opportunity that he possessed.

The irony to the servant's thought process was that he went to great lengths to not lose the talent, but he still lost because the talent was not put to use. He ended up with the same results because of fear. This is a great example to us that we must try even in the face of fear to express that which God has placed in us.

Did you notice how the talents increased? Have you ever experienced learning something new in the process of performing a task? Well that which you learn can be used to increase your skills or the original gift. This is how things have the ability to double and multiply.

Gifts and talents are so important to God. Everything in life has a purpose including you. Your gifts and talents are to be used to help push you further into fulfilling your purpose. You have the same ability in you that God blessed Adam and Eve with when He told to be fruitful, multiply, replenish, subdue, and have dominion on the earth. In every area of your life, you are to have these five things available to operate as they are needed just as Adam and Eve did.

Your gifts and talents are not just for you to enjoy, but they are to be utilized to also help others reach their potential. We all have people who cross our paths to assist us, for us to assist, or to mutually assist each other at the same time. That is the Master's plan.

I pray that you now see the importance of using your gifts and talents and not burying them in the earth. You may have to get a mentor or pursue education to develop your talents, but whatever it takes be willing to do it. Let them come forth to bless and enhance the lives of those that are within your family, your community, and each divine encounter. Remember the punishment suffered by the servant for lack of use?

Take a moment now to think about the things you are naturally good at and the things you enjoy doing. Write these things down and answer the following questions:

1. How many of these things do you have listed that you are currently using?
2. How many of them are not being used?
3. What has stopped you from using them?
4. What plans can you implement today to start using them?

Now it is time to move on to the next chapter to see how we can accomplish this by stepping out of our comfort zones. The only way to do this is to overpower fear and go for it.

CHAPTER ELEVEN

Stepping Out of Your Comfort Zones

The Scriptures say in Zechariah 4:6, *"...not by might, nor by power but by my spirit, saith the Lord of Hosts."* I love this Scripture because it helps me leave the weight and results of my purpose to the Lord God of Hosts, my creator. This helps me to eliminate the process of trying to figure out to complete my purpose and let Him lead and guide me every step of the way.

"Trust in the Lord with all thine heart; and lean not unto thine own understanding. In all thy ways acknowledge him, and he shall direct thy paths" (Proverbs 3:5-6). This passage of Scripture is very crucial and provides a profound truth for the need to really trust God and allow Him to order our steps.

Today many people struggle with change, not only in the quality of life, but with life's lessons. We have experienced many traumatic and devastating things over the years like loss of homes, jobs, family members, and even some of our freedoms. But the good news is that all these things will work out for your good as stated in Romans 8:28.

Nothing happens by coincidence. God has you right where He

wants you. This is the place where He is molding you and fashioning you to complete your assigned purpose. Know that in the school called life, each of the things you have experienced and every person you encounter on this journey, are necessary to get you one step closer to the fulfillment of your purpose.

Currently, where you are right now is where you are supposed to be by His divine appointment. Think of it this way: of all the places you could be, you are right where you are supposed to be at this present moment, because He designed for you to be there. When I think of it in these terms, it makes it easier for me to trust in Him and not rely on my own understanding for the results.

There is nothing that the Creator has not foreseen that will occur in your life. For as the Scriptures tell us in Romans 8:29-30:

For whom he did foreknow, he also did predestinate to be conformed to the image of his Son, that he might be the firstborn among many brethren. Moreover whom he did predestinate, them he also called: and whom he called, them he also justified: and whom he justified, them he also glorified.

Absolutely nothing catches God by surprise.

We are creatures of habit and comfort. God will send storms to shake and rock us out of our comfortable places because we have to keep moving forward. We may stop for a brief rest on this journey of purpose, but we can't get stuck there enjoying the view and smelling the flowers.

There is work to be done. I know that as the Father has me moving around fulfilling my purpose, I was in a particular city that has many different walking parks with water. I love the water and I like to spend a great deal of time there.

The way the Father gets me to move is that I will start to sense His peace lifting despite an otherwise enjoyable or peaceful environment. Things will start to feel and become less comfortable for me. Then I am ready to be led to another peaceful place.

You too may have experienced something similar lately. Isaiah 43:19 has been one of my go to Scriptures when relating to coming out of my comfortable place. God states in that Scripture that He will do a new thing and when it springs forth will we not know it.

Often I did not recognize these new things as direction from God until I was pushed to do so. I was so busy looking at what caught my eye in my comfort zone that I stopped paying attention to what was going on around me. Many times this is how things creep up on us unaware. We must always be looking for God's outstretched hand beckoning us to come and follow where He leads.

Becoming comfortable in one place can produce a spirit of complacency. This mindset will cause us to settle into not wanting to do the work required to change and then procrastination will start to become a welcome friend. But these two are deadly adversaries to the walk of purpose. My friend, learn to keep moving and not to force life's storms to propel you to your next destination. Watch for when God is leading you.

I know you can relate to the things that were shared in this brief chapter. I would like for you to stop here for a moment and make a commitment to yourself that from this point on you will not let yourself get comfortable or complacent as you move to fulfill your purpose. Agreed?

Failures and setbacks are our necessary teachers when it comes to growth and maturity. When we move to the next chapter in this book we will see the proper attitude to have when we supposedly fail or things happen to stop our progress.

CHAPTER TWELVE

Failures and Setbacks

Failures are seen as negative experiences without good results. They help us discover many valuable lessons and they reinforce the path of what not to do. Walking this road to fulfill our purpose, we will experience many failures, roadblocks, and setbacks. We are to look at the lessons and experiences that no one will be able to take from us and apply them to our lives as we go forward.

Don't be that person who tries to avoid failure, but instead be the one who is not devastated by it when it happens. Know that all things are part of the process to mature us to ascend to the next level. I believe there are no coincidences in life, but divine appointments that set us up for the fulfillment of completing our purpose.

People of purpose are not stopped by difficult situations or challenges. They learn to go with the flow because they know their current situation, circumstances, or limitations is only temporary. They are focused and determined to keep moving forward. Actually, the more difficult the situation they face, the more determined they are to overcome it. These people carry the spirit of the Overcomer inside of them. They know that they truly have everything they need to be victorious and successful by digging in and persevering until the storm passes and they are on more solid ground.

There are many stories of people who failed miserably in the beginning of accomplishing their dreams and successes. It is through challenges and failures that true success is born. We have to stay the course if we expect to walk in victory. We cannot give up right at the tip of our breakthrough point.

Failure is like learning how to ride a bike for the very first time. The first time you get on you are guaranteed to fall off at some point. The first time you fall you may say, "Bike riding is not for me", but at that point you have missed out on learning to do something new. When walking out the process of purpose you are going to have these falling or failing experiences. Don't give up at that point. Stay the course until you reach your expected end or desire. Celebrate each victory as it occurs.

Numerous people do not fulfill their purposes in life because their failures and setbacks releases a spirit of fear. This soon becomes a block to protect them from making mistakes. Making mistakes is necessary when walking out our dreams.

The true people of purpose chip away at this fear and press forward using it as momentum to reach their desired goals and to become better educated in the process. We feel exhilarated and alive because we are able to push past these limitations

Another area to conquer when dealing with failure is the area of pride and ego. We tend to want to save face at all cost. Because of pride and ego we do not want to show our imperfections. We believe we have an image to uphold—especially when we are in a position of power and authority.

We all make mistakes. There is no way around making them. Humility is good because it keeps us grounded and coachable by the Holy Spirit. We must rely on Him to get us through these periods of testing. Acts 1:8 tells us that we will be endued with power when the Holy Spirit comes.

Have you ever noticed how your flesh fights to keep from having to experience failure and pain? It will do everything within its power to avoid the many valuable lessons we must learn to move forward in purpose. We can only avoid it for so long, then the inevitable will happen and we will ultimately fail. The silver lining is that we are always protected and we can be ensured that it is very necessary for what lies inside of us to grow.

Failure breeds inspiration and produces wisdom of what not to do when going forward. It is a tried and true method of weeding out the things that do not work because failure is part of the process of cultivating the seed of purpose and moving us forward in our destiny. It is a wise man who can learn from the failures of others and not have to repeat their mistakes.

Learning to embrace failure with the right attitude will produce a more grateful attitude toward life and the purpose that we were sent here to fulfill. Trust God completely as many of the Scriptures tells us that He is worthy to be trusted and He is faithful over His word. We know that His plans will eventually prevail in our lives.

We either can do it the easy way or the hard way. The choice is always ours through the gift of free will. No matter what choice we make, God is still in control.

Now when failure knocks upon your door, I hope you will recognize it as a welcome old friend coming to share its vast wisdom with you. Through failure we become more dependent upon God. Failure is the best teacher for those who press forward to intentionally live out their purpose through the God of purpose.

The next chapter gives us what I like to call our super powers of purpose. I know you are anxious to move forward, but please wait and complete the following assignment.

This chapter discussed how we should handle failures and setbacks.

1. Based on what you learned, I want you to take a sheet of paper and list five things that you recently failed at. Please leave some space so you can complete the next question.
2. Look at these five failures you wrote down and list at least two things you learned from each experience.

Now that you have completed your assignment, you are ready to find out about the super powers in the next chapter.

CHAPTER THIRTEEN

Faith, Commitment, Determination, and Patience

This chapter is very important to the success of fulfilling our divine purpose in life. Without faith, commitment, determination, and patience we will fail miserably and success will definitely elude us every time. These powerful mindsets assist in building the very foundation on which purpose is grown, cultivated, and brought forth to produce the bountiful harvest contained in its seed.

We will look at each attribute separately and collectively throughout this chapter. As we go through the process of purpose, we will see just how important these four are to the very nature of character building that will promote success not only on this leg of the journey, but throughout life. Everything grows as we expand our horizon through knowledge and life experiences.

When purpose is lived out, it becomes contagious and can carry the potential to spark the quest for living purposefully in other people's lives. Through our demonstration and pursuit, we display the characteristics needed for continued success moving forward to our expected end. We become like neon lights or signposts set upon a hill pointing the way to the road less traveled.

Understand that walking out purpose is not a race, but is completed over time. We are encouraged through the word of God that *"the race is not to the swift, but time and chance happens to them all"* (Ecclesiastes 9:11). During the walking out process, the fruit of patience is cultivated and developed to maturing levels. Every step becomes one step closer to the finish line.

God intentionally places things on the pathway to test our willingness and commitment to stay the course and follow His will. These are our times of being led of the Holy Spirit into our wilderness moments, which are a crucial part of our existence. During these times, we must realize that it is only a test and failure is only lurking to teach us valuable lessons and develop new experiences no one can take away from us.

During these wilderness times, we are stripped of things that we have embraced as truth because they were merely only the fulfillment of our fleshly desire to be in total control. This is the place of purification and perfection needed to reach our appointed expected end. We are able to look in the mirror of the soul and see the things that are rising to the top that are no longer necessary to move forward with us down the pathway.

The beauty about this process is that it occurs in repeated cycles. As we continue to mature, we are brought to greater levels of growth. As we continue along the path we are brought more into His likeness and image and less of our natural, carnal selves.

"Faith is the things hoped for, but the evidence of things unseen" — Hebrews 11:1.

Here is my story of faith. On October 3, 2015, I packed all my belongings, loaded up my SUV with as much as I could safely fit into it without obstructing my view through the windows. I put the car in drive and headed out on the highway in search of my new beginnings. I was having an Abraham moment.

Prior to making this decision and being obedient to what God had told me to do, He told me I would need to have the faith like Abraham when He asked for the sacrifice of Isaac, like the three Hebrew boys who were thrown in the fiery furnace because they would not bow down to the king, and Daniel when He was thrown in the lion's den because he refused to stop praying to God despite the king's thirty day proclamation.

For about six months straight prior to me leaving, I kept hearing or seeing this Scripture found in Luke 5:4-5, *"Now when he had left speaking, he said unto Simon, Launch out into the deep, and let down your nets for a draught. And Simon answering said unto him, Master, we have toiled all the night, and have taken nothing: nevertheless at thy word I will let down the net."* The part that really stood out to me was the part that says 'nevertheless at thy word I will let down the net.'

You see, I am a firm believer in when God says something, He has the power to back it up. I left my past behind and I was ready to move in the answered prayer that He was starting to orchestrate in my life. There were many events that transpired prior to me getting to the point of actually making this significant and strategic move of faith.

Faith is a crucial element in fulfilling your purpose. Without it you will not be able to remain committed, determined, or patient. He has led me through three states so far, Alabama, Florida, Georgia, and now I am back in Florida again. The interesting part was that it took a great deal of faith to continue following the cloud and obeying His commands.

Many of the people who hear my story think that I am a little crazy or a truly determined person. I am loving what God is doing for me as I stepped out in faith and trusted Him. Yes, there were some moments of uncertainty on my part, but He would always send someone to encourage me or give me a Scripture to help me stand my ground.

No matter what it looks like and no matter how I may feel about it, I have made up my mind (determination) to go with Him all the way. I am holding on until I see the manifestation of His promises to me as I walk in my purpose. I am at the point it is all or nothing, but failing to complete my task is not an option.

I share this with you because many of you are like me coming out of the boat and walking on the water of faith, commitment, determination, and patience. We are like Peter walking on the water, but we will not look at our surroundings that will cause us to sink. We have to keep our full confidence in the plans He has for us.

He says in Jeremiah 29:11, "*For I know the thoughts that I think toward you, saith the Lord, thoughts of peace, and not of evil, to give you an expected end.*" Meditating on this Scripture helps to strengthen your resolve to keep moving forward. It is for your greater good and those you are sent to influence, plant seeds in, and spark the necessary fires to get them moving forward in their purpose.

It takes faith, commitment, determination, and patience on a daily basis until you complete the level you are on. Rest and be prepared to keep moving. It will not be complete until you have reached your expected end.

He is going to and is showing Himself mighty to those who dare to believe He is God as stated in Hebrews 11:6. Know that He is the greatest reward and fulfillment of life that one can have and possess at any given point in time. It is all in what you are willing to give up to accomplish having Him in this way.

This book and becoming an author was always a dream of mine.

Finally, I have been given the courage and commitment to make this dream a reality. You are my living witness, because you hold the evidence of my dream in your hand or you are reading it online.

Believing in your seed of purpose and nurturing it with determination and commitment will eventually help you become like those people whom you have admired and compared yourself to, but with the thought that your seed expression is just as valuable as theirs. You too have something so valuable to express that the world has waited so long to receive.

Isn't it funny how many things that seem separate are really connected together? As I sat and pondered what this chapter would be about, I discovered that determination has to be a place of no return. It is all or nothing. To explain this concept further. Perhaps, you may have heard people say, "Get in the zone" or "I was in the zone." This is where we have to be when fulfilling your life's dreams and goals. Being in the zone is where determination kicks in. This is the place where you will not come up short and where complete failure is not an option to stop you from moving forward.

In the book of James the first chapter and the fourth verse it talks about letting patience have her perfect work in us. God knows how to make us wait to develop patience in us. Sometimes, the wait can seem unbearable. But it is in this place that He is maturing this fruit of the Spirit.

When fulfilling our purpose it is imperative that we wait on God because He knows the perfect time for us to release our gift in the earth. If we get ahead of Him we will cause great damage.

God will change your day when He wants you to walk according to His plan because He has a certain time for you to do a certain thing. The word says that the steps of a righteous man are ordered by God (Psalm 37:23). It is not anything that I do on my own to be righteous, but it is His righteousness in me that makes me righteous.

We must be committed to do it God's way and patient to do it in His time. He is the one with the power, resources, and the connections that will bless us and help us bless others to do what they have been assigned to do. God will test you to see how committed you are to completing the task by the spirit of patience.

Commitment will help you stay planted until God says it is time to move. I have had many instances out here on this journey where I was starting to get antsy and wanted to do my own thing, but God would quickly remind me He was in control.

I hope that you see how these four super powers work and how they are to assist you in completing the fulfillment of your purpose. Each of them work in conjunction with God's plan and with keeping you on the right track.

In the upcoming chapter we will learn about divine timing and connection, which we have briefly touched on here. I think by now you know the drill that there is an assignment to complete before you should move on.

Your assignment for this chapter is to find an instance when you stepped out in faith. I want you to reflect on this time and see if you had determination, commitment, and patience in the scenario. If you didn't, do you now see why they are important?

Once you finish your assignment, God and I will be waiting for you on the next page. See you there!

CHAPTER FOURTEEN

Divine Timing and Connections

People of purpose value every second of time. They are determined to make every second count. They value time because they know that once it is gone there is no way to get it back. They view time as an investment that must bring back a great return.

When we get into a place where we are not sure what steps to take or what direction we should go, learn to totally rely on His leading. If we choose incorrectly, we can rest assured that He will get us back on the right path.

Settling down in Him has helped me when standing at a crossroad on my path to fulfillment. This is a step in growing strong, unwavering faith. If the decision turns out unfavorable to us, it still provides valuable lessons to be learned.

Open heavens are opening for people who believe in the truth of His word. When you do not hear His voice in response to your prayers it does not mean He is not there. He is merely waiting for you to get in position to receive the answers.

This is God's divine timing. God is always about the perfect time before He moves or speaks. Many things have to come into alignment so that His ultimate plan can move forward. It is in the wait that many people give up and miss out on obtaining their dreams. If Joseph had given up when he was unjustly imprisoned, where would the children of Israel be in their time of famine? Trust God's timing for the fulfillment of your purpose. Learn to be faithful to His instructions and methods by constantly seeking His face.

A valuable lesson to learn is that all things have a timing. Solomon declares this in Ecclesiastes 3:1, *"To every thing there is a season, and a time to every purpose under the heaven."* As you read this book know that your season for your purpose is now. You have been divinely appointed to read it as I was divinely appointed to write it.

Everything is a seed that must be nurtured to grow. The process that grows the seed to the place where it can bring forth fruit is the element of time. God is the creator of time and only He has the power to redeem it.

I am amazed at how some days the time moves slow and then some days it speeds up so quickly. He knows the right mixture of time to get us to our appointed destinations. Many times I used to get upset when I needed to get to a place at a certain time, but things happened to cause me to get delayed. He started to show me that I may have avoided a traffic back up or accident or He was delaying me so that I would arrive on time for a divine connection

God took me on an adventure once when He told me to get dressed and jump in the car. Once I got in the car He directed me every step of the way. He told me I would know my final destination once I saw it. Now this involved a certain level of trust. You might be saying to yourself, "God will really do that?" My answer to you is yes, He can based on what He desires to teach you in your relationship with Him.

As He proceeded to tell me where to drive and turn, I was still unsure of where He was leading me. He patiently kept telling me I would know it when I saw it. Once I was close to my destination, He told me to look to my left and there stood a church painted in my favorite color, purple. The interesting thing was that it had the same name as the last church I had attended before it was closed down.

At the end of the church service I met with the Pastor. God led me to pray for him and give him a word of encouragement. I share this story with you because divine timing and connections start with trusting God to lead and guide your every step, while you are being obedient to His commands. You never know how He will use you to impact a person's life. He knows and orchestrates the right time when the divine connections will surface. It is all dependent upon when everything involved is ready to be connected.

It takes patience to operate on this level. This is where many people miss the mark. You see when He says for us to "*Be still, and know I am God*" (Psalm 46:10a). He is letting us know that He is in complete control and that we have to trust His perfect timing. He will give us the green light to move.

God has so many facets to His being yet to be uncovered and discovered by His creation. He does not deal with us the same way twice. I love God's spontaneity. He gives us new experiences, when we are totally submitted to do His will.

Sometimes, He will bring people you have never met and you will instantly hit it off. There are so many things that come from what we call chance meetings. The truth of the matter is that we are being divinely set up. We are on a collision course with a portion of our purpose.

Every day God is moving by His Spirit even when it seems or feels like nothing is happening. We are the workmanship of His hands and He knows that these little chance meetings will have lasting effects not only on those involved, but also on those we are connected to. These brief experiences will last long after we are gone.

It is such a blessing to be used by Him and to know that our lives are in His hands. You are on the right path to fulfill this leg of your purpose. Have you noticed that things have increased in your life? Perhaps, you are being stretched in areas that you never knew existed or you are moving in a deeper level of intimacy that He is now able to use you for your created purpose.

It is all in the Father's hands and He will continue to orchestrate the timing and the connections. He desires for you to completely trust Him and obey what He tells you to do. It only takes faith the size of a tiny mustard seed to move in the face of fear and uncertainty, but He is right there with you every step of the way.

If you haven't experienced a divine connection lately, your assignment is to look out for one because it is on the way. I know that you experience His divine timing every day, because you live in time.

Now we are ready to press into the chapter on Seizing the Opportunity. Are we having fun yet? I hope your answer is yes, but to all the nay sayers, I say hang on it gets better later. See I made you laugh. Ha! Ha! Ha!

CHAPTER FIFTEEN

Seizing the Opportunities

Various opportunities are contained in our seeds of purpose. Each one is geared to produce the results needed to bring it forth in each season of our life. Unfortunately, we can have a negative impact on the successful outcome of the fruit to be produced by it.

Every day we are presented with opportunities that make us come out of our comfort zones. Many turned into missed opportunities because of the fears of rejection and failure associated with the spirit of pride. It is time to walk in the mindset that no matter if I fail or succeed, the best part of the journey is learning and experiencing something new.

There are valuable lessons to be gained and learned. Knowledge, whether deemed good or bad, is there to broaden your horizon and propel you forward in the process of fulfilling your purpose. The Master Creator knows the outcome of every step, thought, and action you take along this journey and He has already compensated for the choices you will make in life.

If you never try, you will never find out what potential is lying dormant inside of you. Successful people are people who overcome fear and failure by first taking a leap of faith and determining the risk. In the face of apparent failure they don't quit or give up at the first sign of difficulty. They keep trying until they accomplish their desired goals.

Earlier I talked about the talents that the nobleman gave to his three servants. I want to further iterate that premise by this Scripture found in Luke 19:13. *"And he called his ten servants, and delivered them ten pounds, and said unto them, Occupy till I come."*

This Scripture depicts an opportunity presented to these ten servants. They each started with a pound. This is the same with each of us. No matter what our experiences are or have been, we all start with the same things—a purpose to fulfill. It is up to you, just like it was up to these servants to handle the opportunity given to them.

There were some people who refused to let this nobleman rule over them. Out of these ten servants, only two seized the opportunity that they were given. It is a small number of people who will actually capitalize on the opportunities that are presented to them.

God in His infinite wisdom through His inspired Scriptures, helps those who will take heed and follow His commands. Let His word be *"a lamp unto your feet and a light unto your path"* (Psalm 119:105). Just like the example of the ten servants, He is going to test you every step along the pathway to fulfill your purpose

Again opportunities present themselves every day, but we have to have a mindset of I can do it and believe that we can in order to be successful. Faith is a crucial point in walking out the journey of purpose. The Scriptures tell us to:

Have faith in God. For verily I say unto you, that whosoever shall say unto this mountain, Be thou removed, and be thou cast into

the sea; and shall not doubt in his heart, but shall believe that those things which he saith shall come to pass; he shall have whatsoever he saith — Mark 11:22b-23.

Faith will produce variable results every time you exercise patience to wait it out. The testing of your faith is produced through patience. You must not doubt according to the Scriptures if you want to have the results that you desire and are destined to receive. Desire coupled with faith is an unbeatable force.

Another note is that opportunities may not wait on you to seize them. The window of opportunity only stays open for a short time. Being able to quickly discern and calculate the risks associated with it is a necessary skill that is cultivated over time. Reliance on Holy Spirit is crucial at all times, because He will reveal the things you need to know to avoid trouble and be victorious.

A wise person always learns from missed opportunities and knows how to position themselves to seize the next one. Know that there will always be others coming down the path of purpose. The key is to know which ones are there for the taking and which ones are there for learning through the test.

Seizing opportunities develops a trust and confidence to keep moving forward in the pursuit of your purpose—especially when there are great difficulties or challenges to overcome. As you gain ground, you will start to gain momentum. It is such a rewarding feeling when you know you are on the right path that changes your life and the lives of others. It is a never-ending journey of change and transformation.

As you embark on this journey of purpose, remove the fear, doubt, worry, and any unbelief that may try to come to stop you cold in your tracks. God has placed everything you need in your seed of purpose. The odds are always stacked in your favor.

For before you were born you were given everything that God knew you would need to complete your purpose on this earth. It takes life to teach you what is placed inside your seed of purpose. Now as you grow in your trust, you are better able to live a life worthy of purpose.

Before turning the page to move on, please take a minute to consider both the opportunities that you seized and those that you missed in life. Think about the mindsets that you possessed while you answer the following questions.

1. What opportunities presented themselves to you, but you failed to act on them?
2. Why did you let them pass you by?
3. Did feelings of inadequacy or lack of knowledge prevent you from acting upon them?
4. What feeling did you have when you seized the opportunity and it worked out in your favor?

What does a worthy life look like? God will show us through His word. To find out what He says, turn the page and let's read on.

CHAPTER SIXTEEN

Living a Life Worthy of Purpose

> *So I, the prisoner for the Lord, appeal to you to live a life worthy of the calling to which you have been called [that is, to live a life that exhibits godly character, moral courage, personal integrity, and mature behavior—a life that expresses gratitude to God for your salvation]*
>
> — *Ephesians 4:1 (AMP)*

We are called to live a life worthy of our calling found in the fulfillment of our purpose. This life exemplifies godly character, moral courage, personal integrity, and mature behavior expressing gratitude to God for our gift of salvation. Without salvation we would not be able to walk in these characteristics nor represent God on the earth. We take on the nature of Christ to express the nature of the seed of purpose in us.

This lifestyle is one that can be lonely at times and often misunderstood—especially by those who are closest to us. Because of the magnitude of the seed that we have, many will come to destroy or disturb the work we must complete. It is not a time to get discouraged, but one to dig in deeper and move with a greater resolve to make it to the end.

From a heart in tune with the heart of God we are able to walk as His ambassadors through the process of fulfilling our purpose. Our attitude toward the journey can make it one of ease or hardship. The Father tells us that His joy is our strength and in James 1:2 we are to count it all joy when we fall into diverse temptations.

This lifestyle must be one of love and faithfulness just like Jesus displayed when going to the cross to save mankind. His heart was determined to fulfill the purpose on His life no matter the final outcome. He did what He saw the Father do and said what He heard the Father say. He is the ultimate example that each believer must follow.

As we walk out our purpose, we demonstrate a lifestyle worthy of purpose to instruct others to bear down and live their lives on purpose. We become contagious to those around us when they see the success that comes from being obedient. Even in the face of adversity, challenges, and resistance, we have the power to become role models and influence others through our demonstrations of faith.

The gift of purpose is a privilege given to us by the Father. We must sacrifice and be willing to go the distance in order to produce the fruit contained in our seed. The pruning process can be painful, but it produces an abundance of fruit time after time. Every season there is a cutting away of the dead and rotten things that will stunt our growth.

Perhaps, you may be feeling somewhat insignificant and inadequate toward your current lifestyle. The power residing on the inside of you is greater than any power on the planet. You carry inside you the seed of the Almighty God.

Being a yielded vessel that God can use to promote His will is what living a sold out lifestyle is all about. You see, you have been bought with a price and you are not your own. You are His creation, child, son/daughter, and His prized possession. He is crazy about you and His love is unmeasurable toward you.

He has the power to change the hearts of the people you are assigned to bless with your seed of purpose so they can look past the outward appearance and see you like you may not see yourself. He has the power to change the very words you speak that what is heard is His voice and not yours.

I am always amazed at how people see you when you do not even know they are watching. They will tell you things about yourself that you do not see. This has been happening a great deal to me lately. This is God's power of influence in operation in our lives. Many times God will use me in casual conversation to say just what the person needed to hear, but I do not know or recall what I said that made such an impact on them. He does the same to me, when I am talking to people they will say just what I need to hear at that moment.

It is so much fun to watch God use a vessel to bring forth His plan on the earth. The best part is when they enjoy being used and it is not a burden to them. "*For this is the love of God, that we keep his commandments; and his commandments are not grievous*" (1 John 5:3). It is our love for God that will give us the joy to make our lives worthy of living on purpose in service to Him.

When you love someone, you do not want to bring dishonor to them in any way. You desire to uphold their reputation. As our love for God grows, we find it easier to live a worthy lifestyle to exemplify His very nature of all that is good and perfect—even in times of discipline and judgment.

This spirit of excellence is something that is grown and matured over time, along with the many other attributes we must display when we walk out our purpose by faith. We get the privilege to change lives, because of the change in our life. Have you ever had a friend who still thinks of you as you were before you came to Christ or grew up? This is because they cannot recognize or accept the lifestyle change because the old image of you is still ingrained in their mind.

Fret not, continue to move in the way that you must go to carry out your design purpose created by the hands of the Master Potter. He will not lead you in the wrong path, although it can feel that way sometimes.

Only God knows exactly what type of seed He placed in you. As you walk out your lifestyle that is connected to this seed, you start to see it unfold into that beautiful tender plant that grows up to be a strong plant or tree that bears much fruit for the advancement of the kingdom.

Do not worry if you are not where you think you should be. Let God's love comfort you right now. Think about what an impact your life has had on those you have encountered. If it has produced a negative impact, repent, and ask God to forgive and help you to do better. He is right there with you.

We have covered a great deal in our journey of fulfilling purpose. We are heading down to the home stretch where I will wrap it up in the next chapter. Before moving on, as I have done in previous chapters, I am going to ask you to please take a little pause break.

If you can, I want you to stand up and lift your hands up and give God a shout of praise for getting us this far. Thank Him for His love toward you and let Him know just how much you love and appreciate Him.

Take as long as you like in this space of praise and worship. When you are ready, proceed to our final chapter Call to Action.

CHAPTER SEVENTEEN

Call to Action

> *"Being confident of this very thing, that he which hath begun a good work in you will perform* it until the day of Jesus Christ"
>
> — *Philippians 1:6.*

Isn't it a comforting thought to know that the good work that has begun in you by God's mighty hand has been promised to keep working in you until the day of Jesus Christ? To me this shows a continuous cycle of life producing a good work from the seed that He has placed in you before your birth. You are designed with an expected end in mind. The very essence of God's thoughts formulated your life in your mother's womb as He picked out the perfect combination of your mother and father to bring you forth for such a time as this.

I say for such a time as this, because you are still here in this time. Time is relative to the nature of where we are at any given moment. God is the creator of time and all that we know. He can stop or start it. He can speed it up or slow it down. The bottom line is that it is His to do what He wills, just like you are His as well.

When we stop and ponder the billions and billions of people on this planet and everything they do and have on a daily basis, it becomes such an amazement to my mind to fathom. The infinite ruler of it all meticulously put it all together and it manifests at the time He hand selects for things to occur.

You were not an accident but you are part of the grand plan of God's design. You are His seed of purpose on the face of the earth. Jeremiah 29:11 says, *"For I know the thoughts that I think toward you, saith the Lord, thoughts of peace, and not of evil, to give you an expected end."*

You are a thought in God's mind from a place of peace and you will receive your expected end. I am one who always likes to try to figure God out, but the ironic part is I have yet to accomplish that goal. Believe it or not, I still keep trying. I also believe that I am not the only one who tries to do this. Can you relate?

God wants us to love and allow Him to use us to bring others to Him so they too can enjoy His love, peace, and complete freedom. There is a process that we all go through to humble us enough to be used by God. I believe the reason you are reading this book is because you are in that place where you are now pliable on the potter's wheel so that He can mold you into what brings Him pleasure, glory, and honor.

Before Jesus left His disciples, He commissioned them to use their seeds of purpose to spread the gospel unto all nations. We too must ensure that we are spreading the gospel and glorifying God to those we are led to love on and let our seeds bless them with the true light of Christ. We are to plant seeds of encouragement, love, and peace so that they can be nurtured on their journey like He has nurtured us on ours.

I pray that what is written in these pages has encouraged you to fulfill the purpose in your life without any more reservations or resistance. God has a plan designed with you always in His mind and heart. You are special more than you will ever be able to imagine.

On this journey, we have walked through many aspects of what is contained in the seed of purpose and what we face when we try to walk it out. But we are conquerors because that is what is contained in the seeds we carry. Relax and enjoy the ride as the Father pushes you along the path that He has ordained for your life.

Remember you are not your own, but you have been bought with a price. Cast your cares on the One who cares for you (1 Peter 5:7). He loves you with an everlasting and eternal love that is unconditional, but very intentional to the grand plan by including you in the bigger picture for all creation.

It is a privilege to be used by God in whatever capacity He sees fit. Do not despise humble beginnings and remember to multiply your talents so that in the end of it all He can say to you is, *"Well done thou good and faithful servant" — Matthew 25:23.*

I want to thank you for taking the time to read this book in its entirety. I have prayed over every word and asked the Father to let them bless and strengthen you in a supernatural way. I believe it is time to truly be transformed like Peter, James, and John on the mount of transfiguration. We are to exemplify Jesus in all that we think, say, and do so that we can destroy the powers of darkness in our world.

Father, I pray for the readers of this book that You will be with them every step of the way. Let Your word be a lamp unto their feet and a light unto their path. Let them truly understand and allow You to grow the seed of purpose that dwells within them through the revelation and wisdom of Your word. John 6:63 says, "It is the spirit that quickeneth; the flesh profiteth nothing; the *words that I speak unto you, they are spirit, and they are life." Amen.*

Walk in purpose on purpose through the God of purpose in you.

Love you family!

Special Thanks

I want to say a special thank you to my editor, Pam Lagomarsino, who was a pleasure to work with and who diligently took the time to allow God to use her to put the polish on the words He gave me for you.

ABOUT THE AUTHOR

L. J. Boulding is a humble servant, who is a worshiper chasing after the heart of God. She has been a deliverance minister since April 2009, specializing in inner healing for women who have been traumatically abused and hurt through their relationships. She is a Prophet, Seer, and Teacher. She flows in the gifts of prophetic intercession and strategic warfare. Formally, she has been a Youth Pastor, Choir Director, Sunday school and Bible study teacher. The ministry that God is currently birthing through her to oversee is Kingdom Builders for God Healing and Restoration Ministries. If you would like her to know how this book has impacted your life or you would like to contact her please email her at kbfg55@yahoo.com.

54053447R00063

Made in the USA
Charleston, SC
22 March 2016